Crazy Quilt

ALSO BY JOHN TRAIN

In a Japanese hotel: you are invited
to take advantage of the chambermaid.

Crazy Quilt

Remarkable Comic Confusions

including
Sinister Dishes and Weird Arrangements
High Life
Bureaucracy Gone Mad
Antilogies
and Other Threats to Public Order

by John Train

Illustrated by Pierre Le-Tan

HarperCollins*Publishers*

HarperCollins books may be purchased for educational, business, or sales promotional use. For information please write: Special Markets Department, HarperCollins Publishers, Inc., 10 East 53rd Street, New York, NY 10022.

FIRST EDITION

Designed by Nina Gaskin

Library of Congress Cataloging-in-Publication Data

Crazy quilt: remarkable comic confusions including sinister dishes and weird arrangements, high life, bureaucracy gone mad / by John Train; illustrator, Pierre Le-Tan.—1st ed.

    p. cm.
  Includes index.
  ISBN 0-06-017401-3
  1. Anecdotes. I. Train, John.
PN6261.C73 1996
082—dc20   96-12537

96 97 98 99 00 ❖/HC 10 9 8 7 6 5 4 3 2 1

CONTENTS

ACKNOWLEDGMENTS

Some of the items that follow appeared in my "Crazy Salad" column in *Harvard Magazine* over the years. I am grateful for ideas from John Julius Norwich, Charles Chatfield, Frank Cabot, my wife, Francie, and other kind friends; also for the valued advice of Sara Perkins and the patience of Ruth Ann Waite, who prepared the copy.

Crazy Quilt

SINISTER DISHES AND WEIRD ARRANGEMENTS

Ingliz Menu

The waiter brought over a grubby document, creased at the corners and covered with tea stains.

"Ingliz menu," he said, beaming at Laura.

We opened the menu and studied it closely.

Kujuk Ayas Family Restrant
INGLIZ MENUYU

SOAP
>   Ayas soap
>   Turkish tripte soap
>   Sheeps foot
>   Macaront
>   Watcr pics

EATS FROM MEAT
>   Deuner kepab with pi
>   Kebap with green pe
>   Kebap in paper
>   Meat pide
>   Kebap with mas patato
>   Samall bits of meat grilled
>   Almb chops

VEGETABLES
    Meat in earthenware stev pot
    Stfue goreen pepper
    Stuffed squash
    Stuffed tomatoes z
    Stuffed cabbages lea
    Leek with finced meat
    Clery

SALAD
    Brain salad
    Cacik—a drink made ay ay
    And cucumber

FRYING PANS
    Fried aggs
    Scram fried aggs
    Scrum fried omlat
    Omlat with brain

SWEETS AND RFUITS
    Stewed atrawberry
    Nightingales nests
    Virgin lips
    A sweet dish of thinsh of batter with butter
    Banane
    Meon
    Leeches

                    —William Dalrymple, *In Xanadu*

Other Unappetizing Menus

I recently patronized the Subconscious Restaurant in Taipei and the Feeling Café in Verona.

★

The parador in Jaén, Spain, offers SWERDS CHERDE WITH ANALS.

★

The menu of the Mistral Hotel restaurant in Nasebar, Bulgaria, when I had dinner there in September 1994, offered CHICKEN BOWELS.

★

CAFE-RESTAURANT *HAAS* BOCKSTEIN,
On the Elisabeth-Promenade
2 minutes from the terminus of the Bus-Station, a beautiful excursion, from which you will be ravished!

—*Bad Gastein Guide Book*

★

Leo Rosten swears he encountered DREADED VEAL CUTLET on a hotel dining room menu.

★

A Polish hotel restaurant proposes:

SALAD A FIRM'S OWN MAKE

LIMPID RED BEET WITH CHEESY DUMPLINGS IN
THE FORM OF A FINGER

ROASTED DUCK LET LOOSE

BEEF RASHERS BEATEN UP IN THE COUNTRY
PEOPLE'S FASHION

*

The Salongxay Garden Restaurant in Vientiane, Laos, offers these treats:

HALF COOKING MOOSE MEAT

BAKED SCALY ANT-EATER

LAO SAUCE WATER-COCKROACH

*

Eminent philologist J. Bryan III reports visiting a restaurant in Korçë, Albania, whose menu offered

MANURE

Comfort Level

Seoul's city authorities received many complaints about taxi drivers who were rude and whose driving scared the living daylights out of passengers. So the city set up a complaint hotline. Now taxis carry a notice on the inside of the rear door advising passengers of this facility. And what do they call it in English? Intercourse Discomfort Report Center.

—*Far Eastern Economic Review*

Tootle with Vigor

From a brochure of a car rental firm in Tokyo:

When passenger of foot heave in sight, tootle the horn. Trumpet him melodiously at first, but if he still obstacles your passage then tootle him with vigor.

Crazy Notices

In a Tokyo hotel:

Is forbidden to steal hotel towels please. If you are not a person to do such a thing is please not to read notis.

*

In a Belgrade hotel elevator:

To move the cabin, push button for wishing floor.
If the cabin should enter more persons, each one should press a number of wishing floor.

Driving is then going alphabetically by national order.

★

In an Austrian ski hostel:
Not to perambulate the corridors during the hours of repose in the boots of ascension.

★

In an advertisement by a Hong Kong dentist:
Teeth extracted by the latest Methodists.

★

In a Bangkok temple:
It is forbidden to enter a woman even a foreigner if dressed as a man.

Far-Darting Porkers

Three hours into an overnight flight from London to Johannesburg a jumbo jet had to return to Heathrow, South African papers reported. At 35,000 feet the 72 pigs in the hold, unaccustomed to high altitudes, had farted with such abandon that the methane triggered a gas alarm.

In a Bangkok temple: It is forbidden to enter a woman even a foreigner if dressed as a man.

Procedure

The Weifang Medical Institute in Shangdong, China, performed its first open-heart operation for television. Unfortunately, there was a tiny trifling glitch. The medical records had gotten jumbled. So the dying heart patient had his tonsils removed—by a trainee surgeon, as it happened—and the fellow with bad tonsils was subjected to open-heart surgery.

Dialogue

Samuel F. B. Morse transmitted to Alfred Vail the first long-distance telegraph message ever sent, on May 24, 1844. Their exchange admirably launched the miscommunication that technology has brought to later generations.

MORSE (in Washington): What hath God wrought?

VAIL (in Baltimore): Yes.

Compassion

Spoken Turkish offers this cool exchange between two observers to a car crash:

"The poor people are covered with blood. I wonder if they're suffering much?"
"I don't think so, since they've fainted."

Film Notes

In a Singapore hotel, I encountered these unappetizing synopses (reproduced in toto) of available TV film fare:

1. *The Young and the Restless*
Guo-Yang suspects the mysterious man is a fugitive by the name of Li-Fei. Ya-Yun tries to arrest him but to no avail.

2. *Ride the Waves*
Patriach Hua suffers a sudden heart attack. Dr. Jia Xuan is engaged to treat Zhenbang.

Blastoff

One hot summer, Christos Bertos of Corfu had the valuable idea of attaching an oversize fan blade to an old aircraft engine in the hope of cooling down his home. He succeeded. The blast of air blew the roof right off.

Jetsam

A British Automobile Association list of objects abandoned by hotel guests includes a sack of poisonous snakes, a stuffed baby elephant, the cremated remains of a relative, forty-seven vibrators, fifteen blow-up dolls, and a pair of strawberry-flavored edible underpants.

HIGH LIFE

Hand Baggage

Memorandum exchanged between Charles II and his High Chancellor, Lord Clarendon:

KING: I would willingly make a visite to my sister at Tunbridge for a night or two at farthest, when do you thinke I can best spare that time?

CHANCELLOR: I know no reason why you may not for such a tyme (2 nights) go the next weeke, about Wednesday, or Thursday, and returne tyme enough for the adjournement, which yett ought to be the weeke followinge. I suppose you will goe with a light Trayne.

KING: I intend to take nothing but my night bag.

CHANCELLOR: Yet, you will not goe without 40 or 50 horses!

KING: I counte that parte of my night bag.

—Bodleian Library, Oxford (Arch.F.c.4a.f.54)

"Couvrez-vous, Mon Cousin"

The ducal family of Lévis intimates that it is the oldest in Christendom. Their chateau is said to have contained a picture of the Flood, showing Noah carrying a box labeled "Archives of the House of Lévis" into the Ark, and another depicting an early ancestor bowing and doffing his *chapeau* to the Virgin, who is saying, "Please put your hat back on, cousin."*

The New Rolls

The Earl of Mowbray describes the adventure of a friend of his, a commander in the Royal Navy, who saw an ad in the *Times* offering a Rolls-Royce in good condition for the price of five pounds. He instantly telephoned the offerer. A butler answered and put on her ladyship, the owner, who told him in complaisant tones that indeed the car was for sale and why didn't he come around to have a look?

He did. The Rolls was in excellent condition, had less than ten thousand miles on the clock, and was waxed to a mirror finish. The owner was a middle-aged woman, obviously well off, showing

*See Sir Walter Scott's *Journal* of April 9, 1829, upon receiving the Duc de Lévis's *The Carbonaro; a Piedmontese Tale* (2 vols., London, 1829).

no sign of unworldliness. After signing the appropriate papers and paying for and taking possession of the machine, he asked her how it came about that she was letting it go for so little.

Her husband had died recently, she said, and in a late codicil to his will, of which she was the executor, he had directed that his new Rolls be sold and the proceeds turned over to a certain Daisy, with an address in the East End, a run-down neighborhood of London. She was following the instructions to the letter.

Crumbs from the Upper Crust

Says a frequent guest: "You're staying with Mick and Jerry [Jagger] in France, and everyone comes down to dinner in drag, and it's just huge fun. Masses of people sort of screaming, running in and out of each other's bedrooms, applying makeup to the boys. The English and the Irish—because he adores the mad Irish—love to do this. It's wild upper-class house party behavior. It's nothing kinky or sexual. And Jerry has very much cottoned on to this. She was a truckdriver's daughter from Mesquite, Texas, but she's always done very well at learning the ways of the British upper class."

—*Vanity Fair*

Golf

I was startled to discover that to play golf in Switzerland, that well-ordered country, you are required to possess a *certificat de golfeur*. The conception is more or less that of a hunting license: You don't want incompetents wandering around. To attain this happy condition, you play on a lesser course until you have qualified to be received among the elect, like a dead hero into Valhalla.

Japan

The bedroom window of a British TV journalist resident in Tokyo looked out at a large blank wall across the street. His memoirs describe how, late at night, in virtual darkness, a Japanese tennis enthusiast would often appear and practice whacking balls against this blank wall. So far so good. However, the distinctively Japanese feature of this transaction was that he did not appear in scruffy exercising gear. Instead, in the middle of the night, he bedecked himself in white duck trousers, white shirt, and V-neck tennis jersey, together with white socks and tennis shoes! (This will not surprise connoisseurs of Japanese matters, aware that Japanese who go to indoor golf driving ranges, where you hit a ball into a net, are likely to appear in spiked shoes, plus fours, tweed jackets, and matching tweed caps—as near as possible to a perfect St. Andrew's turnout.)

Master Play

The *International Herald Tribune* describes the 1953 Masters tournament:

One of the competitors, Count de Bendern, found his ball lodged in the bank of a brook. Deciding that he could play the ball, he took off his left shoe and sock and rolled his pants leg above the knee. Then he very carefully planted the bare foot on the bank and stepped into the water with his well-shod foot.

"The look on his face as he realized what he had done was more memorable than his shot."

The Right Thing:
Royal Navy Dinner Etiquette

Entry to Dinner

1. Steward reports to the President of the Mess, "Dinner is served, Sir."
2. President with his guest leads the way into the dining room.
3. Band plays "The Roast Beef of Olde England" (according to the Nelson tradition).
4. This signals remaining officers to escort their guests in to dinner.
5. President takes his place and sits immediately.
6. Others take their seats as they arrive.
7. Steward reports to President, "Officers seated, Sir," and states whether a chaplain is present.

Grace

1. President taps the table for silence.
2. If no chaplain present, the President says grace.
3. Chaplain may be as long winded as he chooses.
4. The normal grace for Presidents is, "For What We Are About to Receive, Thank God."

Rules of Order

Between Grace and the Loyal Toast the following rules prevail:

a) Without the President's permission no one may

1. come in and sit down;
2. leave the table;
3. return to the table;
4. read (except the menu);
5. write;
6. speak to anyone not dining (exception: instructing a steward or receiving a message from him).

b) No diner may

1. commence a course before the President;
2. smoke;
3. utter an oath, use foul language;
4. place a bet or wager;
5. discuss political subjects;
6. talk shop (this does not include matters of general interest about the service);
7. speak in a foreign language;
8. mention a woman's name unless she is a celebrity (this rule doesn't apply when ladies other than female officers are present);
9. mention a specific sum of money;
10. propose a toast.

Discipline

Transgression of the rules will result in the following action:

1. A warning, e.g., "Mr. Finch is warned."
2. A light-hearted opportunity for the culprit to use his wit to exonerate himself.
3. The President may award drinks to any diner he chooses as a fine. Such fines should be honoured in the anteroom after dinner in the beverage of the recipient's preference.

Table Manners

1. Wine and beverages are always serviced from the diner's right.
2. Do not begin a course before the President.
3. The bread roll is on the left. Bread is broken with the hands, not cut with a knife.
4. Diners should sit at the table in an erect manner with hands on the lap when not using table utensils. Avoid resting elbows on the table for long periods unless you have sailed around the horn.

General Guidelines

Unless a speaker has something clever and witty to impart to the table, he is best advised to keep a low profile and not attract attention to himself.

Disruptions of dinner for minor infractions interfere with the digestion and bore the guests.

On the other hand, a really clever and witty comment adds colour and vitality to the occasion.

Speeches, stories, and explanations should normally be left until the end of the dinner, after the toasts.

The Guest of Honour is normally called upon for his address as the *final speech* of the evening. At this point the full courtesy of the diners is expected.

Passing the Port

1. When decanters are in place, the senior steward reports, "The wine is ready to pass, Sir."
2. The President orders, "Remove stoppers, pass the port."
3. The port is passed to the left. Those in charge of the port *do not* help themselves before passing the decanters.
4. The port is passed by sliding the decanter along the table. The practice of never lifting the decanter to pour is *not* a tradition and should not be practised.

5. In the navy we never drink a toast in water as superstition says that the subject of our solicitude will die by drowning.
6. No one may touch his wine until the Loyal Toast.

Toasts

A. Loyal Toast

1. The health of Her Majesty shall be honoured seated in the Wardrooms of HM Ships and Naval Establishments, except
   a) when toasts to foreign heads of state are included, or
   b) when a member of the Royal Family is present unless permission is sought beforehand.
2. Guests, military or civilian, follow the custom of the Naval Mess they are visiting.
3. Naval Officers dining in other Messes observe the traditions of that Mess.
4. All diners raise their glasses and repeat "The Queen," and those with wine drink the Toast.

B. Other Nations

1. When a foreign Officer or Official is being entertained (not on exchange duties), the Vice will propose as the first toast the health of the Head of State of the country to which the visitor belongs.
2. The senior Officer of the foreign guests will propose the Toast to the Queen.
3. National anthems of each country are played.

C. Toasts of the Day

1. After cigars and cigarettes are passed, the President will call upon a Member (often the youngest officer present) to give the Toast of the Day.
2. It is customary for the Officer giving the toast to precede it with a brief and witty preamble, applicable to the toast presented.
3. The Toasts of the Day are Monday to Sunday: Our Ships, Our Men, Ourselves, A Bloody War or Sickly Season, A Willing Foe and Sea Room, Sweethearts and Wives, Absent Friends.
4. The Toast of the Day and other toasts are given *standing*.

1. Toasts may be proposed to groups or occasions being honoured.
2. The Chief Cook and Bandmaster are invited by the President to join him in a glass of port and a toast may be proposed.

Adjournment

1. The President announces adjournment for coffee and liqueurs.
2. All diners stand as the President leaves with his guests.

—Posted in Royal Navy Wardroom

A Little Too Much of the Right Thing

Lt. Col. Ian Chant-Stempill from the Gordon Highlanders toasted the health of Lt. Col. Hughie Monro from the Queen's Own Highlanders. The toast was made several times at the request of waiting photographers. Lt. Col. Chant-Stempill was seen to stumble as he left the ceremony.

—*Country Life*

Debugging

Before several colleagues and I set off for Russia to attend a medical meeting, we were warned to be careful of what we said in our hotel rooms—they might be bugged. So as soon as my medic roommate and I arrived, in true James Bond fashion we began a systematic room search for any electronic intruder. We immediately noticed a suspicious bump in the rug. We turned it back to reveal the end of a metal pipe, about two inches in diameter, sealed with a plastic cup. Removing the cup, we found a large nut screwed down on several insulated wires. To deactivate the device, we unscrewed the nut. This was quickly followed by a loud crash in the room below, whose chandelier we'd just unfastened.

—Medical Economics

Homage

What does one offer as a wedding present to a princess? Behold a selection of the tributes displayed at St. James's Palace and pocketed with glad cries by Princess Anne and her husband, Captain Mark Phillips:

NUMBER AND ITEM	BENEFACTOR
499 Three felt mice	Rev. and Mrs. Condor
1242 Talcum powder	Mrs. N. Cleary
1247 Picture postcards of San Diego	Mrs. M. E. Coe
179 Nine 2½p stamps	Mrs. E. E. Gott
294 Book, *Understanding Cystitis*	Mrs. Angela Kilmartin
100 Book, *Settlers of Warsaw*	Mr. Tadeusz Rogala
545 Book, *O World Stop Revolving,* written by donor	Mr. Seyfettin Tunc
285 Novelty handcuffs	Mrs. Valerie Rogers

Accident of Travel

The Bishop of Exeter, William ("Fish") Cecil (1863–1936), traveling by rail to perform a confirmation, misplaced his ticket. "It's quite all right, my Lord," said the conductor, "we know who you are."

"That's all very well," replied the bishop testily, "but without the ticket, how am I to know where I'm going?"

The crisis was resolved by having the conductor keep a sharp watch for the inevitable reception committee.

CULTURE

Lovers' Leap

Scene: San Francisco Opera
Time: 1961
Occasion: Performance of Puccini's *Tosca*

The opera ends as Tosca's lover, the revolutionary hero Cavaradossi, is executed by a firing squad, whereupon Tosca jumps to her death (actually into an invisible net) from the castle wall.

Unfortunately, because of illness, mixups, and the cancellation of the dress rehearsal, the extras who composed the firing squad received only a few words of instruction before marching onstage. How should they get off? "Exit with the principals," they were told—the usual formula. Befuddled, the firing squad shot Tosca. To their amazement it was Cavaradossi who fell dead. And when Tosca, in despair, hurled herself from the battlements, the firing squad, obedient to its instructions, leaped after her into the void.*

*See *Great Operatic Disasters* by Hugh Vickers. Introduction by Peter Ustinov (New York, St. Martin's Press, 1980.)

Boggle

The 1948 movie *Key Largo,* starring Humphrey Bogart and Lauren Bacall, was not shot in Florida at all but in Hollywood (whence such un-Floridian details as fogbanks and gobs of Pacific kelp). The film's success inspired promoters in Rock Harbor, Florida, to change the name of their hamlet to Key Largo in 1952. On the grounds that the new Key Largo was "laden with memories of the great actor," a hotel there bought the decrepit 35-foot launch that appears in a different Humphrey Bogart movie, *The African Queen.* It is suspended on wires over a nearby channel. Signs up and down Route 1 from the new Key Largo proclaim the hotel's Bogart connection. Nearby, a nightclub has arisen called "Bogie's Cafe."

Horrible Poems

On Visiting Westminster Abbey

Holy Moses! Take a look!
Flesh decayed in every nook,
Some rare bits of brain lie here,
Mortal loads of beef and beer.
—*Amanda McKittrick Ros,* 1886–1939

The Valley of Babyland

Have you heard of the Valley of Babyland,
The realms where the dear little darlings stay
Till the kind storks go, as all men know,
And oh! so tenderly bring them away?
                    —*Ella Wheeler Wilcox*, 1850–1919*

When Willie Wet the Bed

Closely he cuddled up to me,
And put his hands in mine,
When all at once I seemed to be
Afloat in seas of brine.
Sabean odours clogged the air
And filled my soul with dread,
Yet I could only grin and bear
When Willie wet the bed. . . .
                    —*Eugene Field*, 1850–1895

Comp. Lit.

It is without regret that I look back at my failure to pursue the study of Comp. Lit. to the bitter end (except for rock band titles, Franglais, and loony

---

*Once described by the London *Times* as "the most popular poet of either sex or any age, read by thousands who never opened Shakespeare."

screen credits). Here, in a piece from *The Times Literary Supplement,* is how we are now supposed to think about *Hamlet:*

> When we come to the last essay of the book, Crapanzano's Saussurean reading of Hamlet as "a semantic crisis," it is tempting to apply it to his distinction between the semantico-referential and the pragmatic. . . . As a consequence of Claudius' murder of King Hamlet, Denmark was plunged into a "semantically de-stabilised world," Crapanzano argues, since the usurper could not serve as a "guarantor of meaning." Under such circumstances, "There is collapse of the meta-pragmatic determination of semantico-referential meaning to both code and context—upon which any adequate social hermeneutic rests . . . the bond of signification between word and thing, signified and signifier . . . is no longer experienced as natural. . . . The sign is sundered; the signifier is cleft from the signified; the word from the thing."

Crazy Writing

George Moore's *Hail and Farewell* describes the wonderfully daft literary collaboration between Yeats, Moore, Taidgh O'Donoghue, and Lady Gregory.

They resolved to write a play on "Diarmuid and Grania." However, they found it hard to agree on a style: it should not be in modern, ancient, or biblical English, nor in Irish dialect, nor in heroic or peasant language, but somehow in an English that suggested early Irish. There was much squabbling. Finally, they agreed. First, Moore would write the play in French.

Then Lady Gregory would translate it into English.

Then Taidgh O'Donoghue would translate that version into Irish.

Then Lady Gregory would translate his Irish back into English.

Then Yeats would "put style upon it."

So Moore got going—"if not in French, in a language comprehensible to a Frenchman."

Trumpery

Donald Trump needs to work on *adjectives* before he can be seriously considered for an honorary D. Litt.

from any substantial institution. To illustrate the problem, here are two exchanges from *Trumped!* by John R. O'Donnell (Simon & Schuster, 1991).

When the media brouhaha over his adultery with Marla Maples exploded, he was surprised but delighted about it.

"Geez, Jack, did you read the papers today? It's just incredible. It's incredible. It's unbelievable what they're printing. . . . This is great for business. I think this is great for business. Don't you? Don't you think this is great for business?"

And when O'Donnell quit his job at Trump Plaza:

"Wait a minute, Donald! . . . I'm fucking sick of you treating these people this way."

"You're fucking sick of it!" he cried. "Well, I'm fucking sick of the results down there, and I'm fucking sick of looking at bad numbers . . . and I'm sick and fucking tired of you telling me no!"

"Donald, you can go fuck yourself!" I cried.

Best Boys, Gaffers, Wranglers

It is astonishing to see how long screen credits have become: many minutes, sometimes. Perhaps one should produce a film to consist *entirely* of credits. And functions are dragged in one wouldn't think required much recognition. I was fascinated, for example, to see among the credits of *A Brief History of Time* someone called the Chicken Wrangler. He was doubtless the invisible figure holding up the bird at the very beginning of the movie.

Here are some more:

1. Moth Wrangler (from *The Silence of the Lambs*).
2. Second Second Assistant Director. (Quite common: it seems nobody wants to be merely a Third Assistant Director.)
3. Second Second *Assistant* Assistant Director (from *Schindler's List*).
4. Cons and Frauds Consultant.
5. Italian Fiscal Representative. (A government tax inspector stationed on the set to make sure you don't pay the Second Second Assistant Director, or whomever, off the books . . . and who is himself doubtless slipped a *bustarella* off the books.)

6. Executive Drag Consultant (from *Priscilla, Queen of the Desert*, which turns on homosexuality).
7. Incomprehensible Franglais screen credits (both from *Le Colonel Chabert*):
   Perchman
   Grapman

The Roar of the Rubbery Fruits

In recent years there has arisen a pleasantly dotty genre: effervescent wine-writing. How about this bit (authentic, I promise) from the London *Sunday Mail* magazine?

And oh, what a confection of delights you find in a glass of this Brouilly! A daisylike floweriness coddled in the almondy scents of a Bakewell tart assaults you at a sniff. There's a rubberiness, yes, as you would expect, but high-class rubber, make no mistake. Take a swig (for, despite the price, this remains essentially a swigging wine), and in roar the cherry fruits. There's a touch of cream, a stab of pepper . . . even a faint edge of cheese. It's a serious example of a marvellously unserious wine.

Libretto

English-language synopsis of *Carmen*, from a performance in Genoa, quoted in a program of the Grand Rapids Symphony Orchestra:

Act 1. Carmen is a cigar-makeress from a tabago factory who loves with Don Jose of the mounting guard. Carmen takes a flower from her corsets and lances it do Don Jose (Duet: "Talk me of my mother"). There is a noise inside the tabago factory and the revolting cigar-makeresses burst into the stage. Carmen is arrested and Don Jose is ordered to mounting guard her but Carmen subduces him and he lets her escape.

Act 2. The Tavern. Carmen, Frasquito, Mercedes, Zuniga, Morales. Carmen's aria ("The sistrums are tinkling"). Enter Escamillio, a balls-fighter. Enter two smuglers (Duet: "We have in mind a business") but Carmen refuses to penetrate because Don Jose has liberated her from prison. He just now arrives (Aria: "Slop, here who comes!") but hear are the bugles singing his retreat. Don Jose will leave and draws his sword. Called by Carmen shrieks the two smuglers interfere with her but Don Jose is bound to dessert, he will follow into them (Final chorus: "Opening sky wandering life").

Act 3. A roky landscape, the smuglers shelter. Carmen sees her death in cards and Don Jose makes a date with Carmen for the next balls fight.

Act 4. A place in Seville. Procession of balls-fighters, the roaring of the balls is heard in the arena. Escamillio enters (Aria and chorus: "Toreador, toreador, all hail the balls of a Toreador"). Enter Don Jose (Aria: "I do not threaten, I besooch you") but Carmen repels him wants to join with Escamillio now chaired by the crowd. Don Jose stabbs her (Aria: "Oh rupture, rupture, you may arrest me, I did kill her") he sings "Oh my beautiful Carmen, my subductive Carmen."

Home on the Range

On billboards in Salzburg and Vienna I encountered posters for a promising pop music combo:

THE LENINGRAD COWBOYS
"We Cum From Brooklyn"

*

BUREAUCRACY GONE MAD

Advise and Consent

"Henry Rose"—ostensibly a radio call-in talk-show host but actually a satirical journalist from *Spy* magazine—interviewed a number of incoming members of Congress on an urgent foreign policy issue: the horrible events in Freedonia (the imaginary situs of that immortal Marx Brothers film *Duck Soup*).

Representative James Talent, Republican of Missouri, took a strong stand.

> QUESTION: What should we be doing to stop the ethnic cleansing in Freedonia?
> TALENT: I think anything we can do to use the good offices of the U.S. government to assist stopping the killing over there, we should do.

Representative Nick Smith, Republican of Michigan, favored a more measured response.

> QUESTION: What should we be doing to stop the ethnic cleansing in Freedonia?
> SMITH: My impression, Henry, is we've gotta be very careful, that moving through the United Nations effort has a great deal of merit right now.

Representative Jay Inslee, Democrat of Washington, was properly concerned.

QUESTION: Do you approve of what we're doing to stop what's going on in Freedonia?
INSLEE: I have to be honest with you. I'm not familiar with that proposal, um, but it's coming to the point now that a blind eye to it for the next ten years is not the answer.

Paperwork I

The *Wall Street Journal* describes how the California State University System ordered one book from the Information Economics Press in New Canaan, Connecticut:

1. The Purchase Order (P.O. #940809) was 8 pages long.
2. The P.O. required that the publisher obtain a determination as to residency or nonresidency for purposes of California tax withholding, such withholding to be reclaimed by filing a year-end California tax return.
3. Thirty-eight percent of the purchase price was to be withheld pending a year-end federal form 1099 for this transaction.

4. The P.O. required the purchaser to submit a Vendor Data Record (Form 204), as well as a Vendor Information Sheet.

5. The P.O. required that the publisher submit a copy of its O.S.M.B. Small Business Certification. (The publisher did not know how to obtain such a certification.)

6. A P.O. rider contained a Privacy Statement carrying $20,000 penalties.

7. The publisher was required to post statements in its place of business notifying its employees of its compliance with Code Section 8355 and of adoption of a Drug-Free Awareness Program, with penalties as specified under California law.

8. The P.O. required an agreement by the publisher to waive any complaint of copyright infringement by employees of the University.

9. The P.O. included a Minority/Women Business Enterprise Self Certification (Form 962), requiring statistics on the ethnic makeup of the publisher's work force.

Since the work force consisted of one husband and one wife, and since the order was for a total of $20, it was suggested that the California State

University System just go out and buy a copy in a bookstore.

Paperwork II

A young patient of mine applied to the Council (*Working for a better tomorrow,* as the mission statement at the bottom of its stationery puts it) for a flat. His mother, he said, hated him, and had threatened several times that she would kill him one day. This was not an idle threat: she had several convictions for assault.

So when my patient told the housing officer that he had to leave home to avoid being murdered by his mother, the officer agreed it was an emergency. All he required before allocating him a flat, therefore, was confirmation in writing from his mother that she intended to kill him at some time in the near future.

—*The Spectator* (London)

Cleanliness Is Next to Godliness

The Environmental Protection Agency determined that the municipal water treatment system of the city of Anchorage must remove 90 percent of the organic materials it handles before the city released its treated water into the ocean.

To achieve this objective, the city had to arrange with local fish processors to dump 5,000 pounds of fish guts into its sewage system every day to give the treatment plant enough to chew on.

Crazy Titles

The Federal Energy Administration put out the following staff memorandum:

SUBJECT: EXECUTIVE TITLES

OMB will shortly place a freeze on the proliferation of FEA titles. In the interest of maintaining staff morale, it has been decided to make the remaining titles available on a limited basis for the next two weeks. Written request and justification for the remaining titles should be filed with the Deputy Associate Assistant Administrator for Management Nomenclature. . . .

Those titles currently in use are

1. Administrator
2. Deputy Administrator

3. Assistant Administrator
4. Deputy Assistant Administrator
5. Associate Deputy Administrator
6. Associate Assistant Administrator
7. Deputy Associate Assistant Administrator

Those titles available for selection during the next two weeks are
1. Associate Administrator
2. Deputy Associate Administrator
3. Assistant Associate Administrator
4. Deputy Assistant Associate Administrator
5. Assistant Deputy Associate Administrator
6. Assistant Deputy Administrator
7. Assistant Associate Deputy Administrator
8. Associate Assistant Deputy Administrator
9. Associate Deputy Assistant Administrator

Each of the Assistant Administrators, Associate Administrators, and so on of the FEA had a description at the end of his title, such as "Assistant Administrator for Enforcement" and "Associate Administrator for International," which led to the wildest of the lot: "Acting Associate Assistant Administrator for Administration." His colleagues called him "5-A."

If the slot had ever opened up, I would have liked to apply, as one keenly interested in names, for the position of Temporary Acting Associate Assistant Administrator for Management Nomenclature Management.

Weekly Abstinence

Notice

By decree dated February 1907 the Rural Police [*Garde Champêtre*] of this commune are required to insure that a weekly marital abstinence [*repos matrimoniale*] is observed in all households, and that no erotic activity [*exercice galant*] is carried out on Sundays and holidays.

All infractions will be punished as prescribed by law.

Isidor Cornandouille
Délégué

Saint-Jean-Du-Gard

I encountered a copy of this proclamation while walking in the Cévennes, the mountains between the Alps and the Pyrenees. Knowing France, I expect it had no effect whatever, and indeed may have inspired the local gentry to redoubled *exercices galants*.

Saving Bruin

Game wardens and wildlife biologists were among those gathered for nearly eight hours on a farm in northwestern Louisiana to save what they thought was a bear 50 or 60 feet up in a pine tree. A veterinarian fired tranquilizer darts at the critter in an effort to get it down. Deputies and wildlife agents strung a net to catch the bear when the tranquilizers took effect. . . .

"People really wanted . . . to help and protect that bear and get him where he was supposed to be," Norman Gordan, the owner of the farm said. . . . It wasn't until the tree was chopped down . . . that they discovered they were rescuing a dart-riddled garbage bag.

—Associated Press

Let a Hundred Flowers Bloom

A division within a Fortune 500 company issued a memo that encouraged employees to increase their global competitiveness by taking foreign-language instruction during the workday. Six months later all those who had availed themselves of the offer were fired. Management had apparently concluded that anyone who had the time to take a course during business hours was obviously underemployed.

—*Fortune,* June 10, 1996

Crazy Finance

Full Explanation

The governor of Malaysia's central bank, Jaffar Hussein, resigned after announcing that the bank had lost 5.7 billion *ringgit* ($2.1 billion) by speculating in derivatives. This loss exceeded the central bank's entire capital and reserves.

"Errors were made," Hussein declared.

Fuller Explanation

Fugitive developer Juergen Schneider borrowed $3 billion and went bankrupt.

"Errors were unquestionably made," Deutsche Bank Chairman Hilmar Kopper declared.

Winter Break

An official of a northeastern city took frequent junkets on "city business." He was accompanied by his secretary in her capacity as a municipal employee.

The secretary was in on all of her boss's doings and, as one of her perquisites, had a key to his safe deposit box, which received regular additions that were not declared to any tax authority.

One winter the pair visited Miami to "represent the city government" at an air pollution conference.

They had a sensational weekend, perhaps too sensational. At the end of it, the politician was carried off by a heart attack.

The secretary checked out of the hotel forthwith, flew north, and at opening time the following morning appeared at the bank with her key to the safe deposit box.

The obituary had not yet run in the local morning papers, so she had no trouble gaining access to the box.

Some days later, when the box was officially opened, nothing was discovered in it except the owner's will and some other documents: no cash.

When the tax authorities questioned the secretary, she said that she hadn't known that a safe deposit box was supposed to be sealed after the owner's death, and had removed only some of her personal papers.

However, among the politician's effects at home were found three more sets of the special keys used for safe deposit boxes. The authorities questioned the secretary about those keys. She knew nothing about them. Aha, the agents replied, he must have been keeping boxes under false names in other cities.

Two words escaped the secretary's lips: "The rat!"*

R.I.P.

Greenville, S. C.—Relatives of a dead man received a letter saying his food stamps would be discontinued because he died, but he can reapply if anything changes.

Al Palanza Jr.'s brother died about two weeks before the letter arrived from the Greenville County Department of Social Services.

"Your food stamps will be stopped effective March 1992 because we received notice that you passed away. May God bless you. You may reapply if there is a change in your circumstances," the letter said.

—Associated Press

* See Jake Fisher (Internal Revenue Service), *Human Drama in Death and Taxes*, New York, 1980.

Learning Curve

The New York City Board of Education maintains 6,000 bureaucrats to run its central office.

The Archdiocese of New York requires a staff of 26 to serve about a fifth as many pupils.*

*See *Reason* Magazine, October 1990.

ANTILOGIES

In every language, some words have a secondary meaning that is the opposite of their primary one. For instance, in both English and French a *sanction* is a form of opposition or punishment, as in economic sanctions, but also permission or even blessing, as of a marriage.

For lack of a term for this idea in English, in writing about it I invented the term *antilogy*. It seems to arise in several ways: first, when words from different sources, bearing different meanings, flow together. As an example, take *cleave*, meaning both to chop apart and to stick together. Its two senses resulted from different Indo-European roots; one gave Old English *cleovan*, split, while the second led to German *kleben*, glue together. Another source is when a word invokes a general idea that itself contains contrary relationships. "I'm renting my house," for example, does not specify whether the speaker is lessor or lessee.

Then, a word's meaning may evolve into a contrary sense, as *elegant* from "opulent" (decoration) to "simplest possible" (mathematical solution), or *liberal,* formerly meaning "opposed to government intervention" but now, in the United States, "in favor of government intervention."

Apparent: Clearly so; an illusion (e.g., "apparent wind" in sailing).

Attraction of (e.g., dogs for men): Attracted to; attracted by.

Bag (it): Capture it; (slang) discard it.

Boned: Containing bones (e.g., corset stays); without bones (e.g., serving of fish).

Buckle: Fasten together; fall apart.

Charterer: Provider; user.

Cleave: Chop apart; stick together.

Contemporary: (Alive) at this time; (alive) at another time. Of a picture frame or the binding of an old book, "contemporary" can mean either the original or a modern replacement.

Continue: Proceed; (legal) put off proceeding.

Critical: Opposed; an essential support (e.g., "His speech was critical").

To a degree: Somewhat; greatly.

Discharge: Reject (waste, or an employee); accept (a commitment).

Downhill: (Particularly going—) getting worse; getting better (e.g., "It's downhill from here on").

Dust: Remove dust; lay down dust (e.g., with cinnamon, or crop-dusting).

Engagement: (Matrimonial) loving tie; (military) battle.

Enjoin: Require; (legal) forbid.

Fast: Moving rapidly; not moving (as make fast or stand fast).

Fight with: Fight against; fight together with.

to Finish: Perfect (e.g., furniture); destroy (e.g., finish off).

Fix: Repair; (colloq.) destroy (e.g., "I'll fix him").

Garnish: Add (e.g., parsley to food); take away (from salary).

Handicap: Disadvantage; advantage (e.g., "I'll give you a handicap").

Heave to (maritime): (of sailor) get going; (of sailboat) halt.

He could care less: (Literally) he might be less concerned; (colloq.) he could not be less concerned.

Horned: Possessing horns; (cattle) with horns removed.

Knockout: Collapse; (colloq.) triumph.

Let: (double antilogy):

(a) Permit; obstruct (as in tennis, and "let or hindrance").

(b) Supply as lessor; use as lessee.

Let him have it: Grant his desire; (slang) murder him.

Liberal: (U.S.) in favor of government intervention; (elsewhere) against government intervention.

Lose no time in . . . : Do promptly; not do at all.

(When sent unsolicited tomes, Henry James is said to have liked to reply, "I shall lose no time in reading your book.")

Marketing: Selling; (household) buying.

Minimum (notably, a minimum commission or order): Least possible; no less than.

Moot (double antilogy):

(a) Under consideration; not under consideration.

(b) Undecided; (law) decided.

Overlook: Watch over; fail to watch over.

Oversight: Supervision; failure to supervise.

Peer: An equal; (colloq.) a superior.

Pinch hitter: Superior substitute (baseball); inferior substitute (all other usages, notably a replacement speaker).

Presently: In the near future; (colloq.) now.

Qualified: Just right (job applicant); defective (approval, auditor's report, etc.).

Quite: Slightly (e.g., "quite nice"); utterly (e.g., "quite out of the question").

Rarely (e.g., skillful): Very good; not very good.

Renter: Landlord; tenant.

Riddler: Propounder of riddles; solver of riddles.

Rock: (e.g., of Ages) solid support; (music) hysterical agitation.

Sanction: Permission; punishment.

Several: Numerous; single (e.g., "joint and several").

Stand: Stay still; move (e.g., stand out to sea, or for Parliament).

to Strike: Act; (labor) stop acting.

Table (parliamentary): Bring up for discussion; defer discussing.

Temper: Harden; soften (e.g., justice with mercy).

Terrific: Repellent; (colloq.) attractive.

Throw out (idea): Propose; reject (e.g., baby with bathwater).

To my knowledge: I know; I don't know.

to Top: Increase (e.g., a record, or added whipped cream); decrease (e.g., a tree).

Trim: Cut down; embellish (e.g., turkey or Christmas tree).

Unbending: Rigid; easing off from rigidity.

Untouchable: Eminent beyond criticism; at the bottom of the heap.

Wicked: Deplorable; (colloq.) admirable (e.g., "a wicked serve").

Wind up: Prepare to start (pitchers and watches); prepare to stop (companies).

You can't be too . . . (e.g. prudent): You should be as prudent as possible; don't be excessively prudent.

British

Action: Activity; inactivity (an "industrial action" is a strike).

Chuffed: Pleased; irritated.

Down: Low; high place.

Mothering: Mother's attentions to child; child's attention to mother, notably Mothering Sunday (corresponds to U.S. Mother's Day).

Not half: A little; (colloq.) a lot.

Anglo-American

Are you through? (telephone operator): Are you ready to stop talking? (U.S.); Are you ready to start talking? (U.K.).

Bomb (of play, etc.): Disaster (U.S.); triumph (U.K.).

French

Bestial: Horrible; (colloq.) wonderful

Combattre avec: Fight against; fight together with.

Farouche: Ferocious; timid.

Hôte: Host; guest.

Louer: Be lessor; be lessee.

un Malheur: A failure; (colloq.) a success.

Mortel: Extremely boring; (colloq.) delightful.
Salut: Hail; farewell.
Sanctionner: Permit; forbid.
Vaquer: Be unoccupied; be occupied.

Latin

Altus: High; deep.
Con (prefix): With; against.
Lentus: Stiff; pliant.
Recludo: Close; open.
Sacer: Holy; accursed.
Tollo: Raise up; cast down.

BUSINESS DIRECTORY

DOCTEUR ACHE, DENTISTE
　　Attaché d'Enseignement à la Faculté
　　de Chirurgie Dentaire, Paris

ARGUE & PHIBBS, SOLICITORS
　　Albert Street, Sligo, Ireland

BRIGADIER ATTACK, MINISTRY OF DEFENSE
　　Director of Army Management Services
　　Civil Service Yearbook 1980

NOVELLA BOOKER, LIBRARIAN
　　Brooklyn, New York

CHEATHAM & STEELE, BANKERS
　　Wallowa County, Oregon

MR. CLAPP, VENEREAL DISEASE COUNSELOR
　　County Health Service
　　San Mateo, California

CLIMAX UNDERWEAR CO.
　　Cincinnati, Ohio

DR. CROAKER, PATHOLOGIST
　　University of Florida School of Medicine

DR. AND DR. DOCTOR
Westport, Connecticut

DR. I. DOCTOR, EYE DOCTOR
Ferndale, Michigan

DOOLITTLE & DALLEY, ESTATE AGENTS
Kidderminster, England

DR. DOTTI, PSYCHIATRIST
Rome, Italy

DERAIL EASTER*

DR. FANG, DENTIST
Tillman Clinic
Belmont, Massachusetts

LAWRENCE J. FELONY, JUSTICE
Commonwealth of Massachusetts
Cambridge Division
District Court Department of the Trial
Court

WALBURGA FLOSS, DENTAL TECHNICIAN
Munich, Germany

*Chicago motorman whose train went off the tracks in 1979.

MR. FORECAST
Assistant Director, Social and Regional
Statistics
U.K. Civil Service Yearbook 1980

FUZZEY TELEVISION LTD.
St. Peter Port
Guernsey, Channel Islands

THE GENUINE IMITATION JEWELRY CO.
Hong Kong

KATZ PAJAMA COMPANY
New York, New York

DR. DEBRA KROAK
Tucson, Arizona

DR. BUM SUCK LEE, UROLOGIST
Newark, New Jersey

TERROR LEKOTA, ANTI-APARTHEID ACTIVIST
South Africa

CHRIS MOLAR, D.D.S.
Loyola Dental School

V. NIKITIN*
> Head of State Procurement Commission for Tobacco

W. T. ODOR, PLUMBER
> Corpus Christi, Texas

FATHER O'PRAY
> Church of St. Ignatius Loyola
> New York, New York

DR. ZOLTAN OVARY, GYNECOLOGIST
> New York Hospital
> New York, New York

SCOTT PARADISE
> Episcopal Chaplain

PLUMMER & LEEK, PLUMBERS
> Sheringham, Norfolk, England
> (London *Times*)

DR. DAVID P. STIFF, PATHOLOGIST
> St. Vincent's Pathology Consultants
> Bridgeport, Connecticut

---

*Dismissed by Gorbachev, who blamed him for cigarette shortages—*New York Times,* August 31, 1990

MANNERS, MORALS, AND RELIGION

Getting Things Straight

Had I been present at the creation, I would have given some useful hints for the better ordering of the universe.

—Alfonso X (the Learned) of Spain

O Tempora

Anthony Accetturo, 55, a top Lucchese crime family leader turned government witness: "The new generation that is running things threw all the old rules out the window. The key word is greed. All they care about is money, not honor."

—*Fortune*

Moonstruck

A student at the University of Idaho, Jason Wilkins, undertook to moon passersby from his window on the third floor of a dormitory. To that end, he pressed his naked buttocks firmly against the glass—too firmly. Moments later he hurtled into the void, crashing to the concrete three stories down.

In due course Master Wilkins and his parents filed suit for $940,000 against the state, claiming negligence.

Haggle

A quarrel between Australian business partners in Sydney turned ugly when one man had part of his nose bitten off after sinking his teeth into the other's thumb.

—Financial Times

The First Conviction for Obscenity

Legal pundits are agreed that the earliest reported case on obscenity is dated 1663 and is that of the King *v.* Sir Charles Sedley.

Accompanied by Charles Sackville . . . Sedley and Sir Thomas Ogle engaged in a drinking spree at "The Cock," Oxford Kate's tavern in Bow Street by Covent Garden. Having achieved that degree of ecstatic inebriation which releases inhibitions, they mounted to the balcony of the tavern and, as Johnson dryly puts it, "exposed themselves to the populace in very indecent postures."

Sedley was bolder. Naked as a jay, he harangued the hundreds of amazed men and women; captured their attention; preached a mountebank sermon; shouted, according to the ubiquitous Pepys, that he had for sale such a powder as would cause all women to run after him; and culminated with rich profanities that "aroused publick indignation. . . ."

He was fined two thousand marks, committed without bail for a week, and bound to his good behavior for a year, on his own confession of information against him, "shewing himself naked in a balcony, and throwing down bottles (pist in) vi & armis among the people in Covent Garden, contra pacem and to the scandal of the Government."

A flimsier, more appallingly pointless foundation for the superstructure of law that was later erected could hardly have been deliberately laid.

—*Harvard Law Review**

---

* Looking into this unedifying episode, I find that according to Anthony Wood, "Sir Charles Sedley being fined . . . he made answer that he thought he was the first man that paid for shitting—thus giving another slant to the juridic aspect."

Correcter Than Thou

Rejecting subsidized student tickets to *Romeo and Juliet*, headmistress Jane Brown of the Kingsmead Primary School in Hackney, East London, excoriated the play as "entirely about heterosexual love."

Modester Than Thou

A sign at an African mammal exhibit in Washington's Smithsonian Museum apologizes for giving the impression that humans are "more important" than other animals.

Bug Off

Gerome Norman, store proprietor in Sydney, Australia, swatted a bothersome mosquito . . . and got him! Hearing of this, animal rights activists promptly picketed the shop.

A Successful Lawsuit

. . . from the lawyer's standpoint, that is.

The First National Bank of Boston was sued in a class action case, and lost. Pursuant to the judgment, the bank was required to deposit the sum of $8.76 in the account of each member of the class.

The court then allowed $8.5 million in lawyers' fees, to be payable, naturally, by the victorious plaintiffs.

As a result, $90 was *withdrawn* from each account that had just received $8.76, representing a net loss of over $80 per depositor as a result of this successful litigation.

A number of unhappy plaintiffs then sued their lawyer, but got nowhere. To add to their misery, their lawyer has sued *them*—his own clients—for an additional $25 million on the grounds of "malicious prosecution."*

*See the *Wall Street Journal,* April 3, 1996.

Lawyers' Bill in
King Case Stirs Wonder

Los Angeles—The 23 lawyers who formed Rodney G. King's legal team have submitted their bill to the City of Los Angeles, and it's a whopper: $4.4 million in legal fees for 13,000 hours of work, at up to $350 an hour.

The bill is $600,000 more than the $3.8 million that Mr. King received in his judgment against the city.

Among the more than 100 pages of particulars, presented to the court at a hearing on Monday, are $1,300 to accompany Mr. King to a movie, $1,625 to a play, and $650 to attend his birthday party.

—*The New York Times*

Fair Warning

Ministère de L'intérieur
Police Nationale

Signs Used by Vagabonds and Thieves
[On the fence outside your house]

× Burglary already planned.
◊ Empty house.
/// House already visited.
△ Single woman.
○ No use trying.
⊕ Nothing of interest.
ᴆ Generous people.
ᴔᴔ Very good prospect.
⊕ Good reception if one talks about God.
⊐▨▨ Dog.
⊐ Work available.
⊽ Tender-hearted women.
⊓⊓ Steer clear of this town.
⧯ Vigorous police in this town.
⬦ Occupant has an official position.
⊑⊒ Timorous person.

Happy Ending

An Israeli hitchhiker was impregnated by a driver who picked her up. After three years she tracked him down and demanded child support.

The driver and his wife had no children, although they had been married for twenty years, so the father sued for custody. The Supreme Court of Israel determined that he was indeed better qualified than the mother to raise the child and granted his demand.

Intimation

Senator William M. Stewart of Nevada engaged Mark Twain as his secretary.

The Episcopalians of Nevada asked Stewart to introduce a bill incorporating their church. The senator told Mark Twain to answer that this was a state, not a federal, matter.

Mark Twain was not overly dedicated to religion. His letter to the Episcopalians in response to their request took a very high line indeed.

"You will have to go to the State Legislature about this little speculation of yours—Congress don't know anything about religion. But don't you try to go there, either; because this thing you propose to do out in that new country isn't expedient—in fact, it is simply ridiculous. Your religious people there are too feeble, in intellect, in morality, in piety—in everything pretty much. You had better drop this."

This tone proved typical of Mark Twain's letters. One day the senator shouted, "Leave the house! Leave it forever!" Mark Twain later wrote that he "regarded that as a sort of covert intimation that my services could be dispensed with, and so I resigned."

Revelation

QUESTION: What is the religion of the Italians?
ANSWER: They are Roman Catholics.
QUESTION: What do the Roman Catholics worship?
ANSWER: Idols and a piece of bread.
QUESTION: Would not God be very angry if He knew that the Italians worshipped idols and a piece of bread?
ANSWER: God *is very* angry.

—*"Near Home, or Europe Discovered,"* 1850

Intercession

Prayer by John Ward, sometime M.P. for Weymouth:

O Lord, Thou knowest that I have lately purchased an estate in fee simple in Essex. I beseech Thee to preserve the two counties of Middlesex and Essex from fire and earthquake: and as I also have a mortgage at Hertfordshire, I beg of Thee also to have an eye of compassion of that county, and for the rest of the counties. Thou may deal with them as Thou art pleased. O Lord, enable the bank to answer all their bills and make all my debtors good men, give a prosperous voyage and safe return to the *Mermaid* sloop, because I have not insured it, and because Thou hast said, "The days of the wicked are but short," I trust in Thee that Thou wilt not forget Thy promise, as I have an estate in reversion which will be mine on the death of the profligate young man, Sir J. L.

LANGUAGE

Pronouncement

INVOCATION

O muse of doggerel, help us *traverse*
The hazards of polite palavers.

Here, then, are thoughts that came to me
as I was strolling on the *quay.*
First, while pronunciation varies,
we should try to say *vagaries.*
And honor him who has the cheek
to be a member of the *clique*
of those who, when they make a face,
describe it as a wry *grimace*
(although we should avoid the boor
who always keeps his visage *dour*).

Our learned friends we may embarrass
should we fail to call it *harass.*
Please poke a sharp stick in the eye
of anyone who speaks of *i-*
talics. May he suffer *chas-*
tisement who puts a "shush" in *gas-*
eous. Sue the ignoramus who

says "you" instead of "oo" in *cou-*
pon (but extol the happy few
wise enough to sound the "you"
in *cupola* and *culinary*). Zap
whoever won't accent the *app*
in *applicable*. Flog and flay
those whose felonies are *hei-*
nous. Kindly always grant *prece-*
dence to the lengthy E in *cre-*
dence. Those who fail to stress the *aff*
in *affluent* commit a gaffe.

Keep your distance from the guy
that spreads the itch of *impeti-*
go. Silver lines each Wall Street storm
for plungers bold whose wealth is *form-*
idable; is it brains or fate
that determines such men's *stat-*
us? A bite is better than a bark
for him who drops the C in *arc-*
tic. Throw the nitwit for a loss
who emphasizes "pit" in *hos-*
pitable. And please cast a hex
on oafs who fail to call it *ex-*
quisite (and *explicable*). A coffin
for the T in *of(t)en* and in *sof(t)en*.

Down with wretched old King Zog,
who rightly skulked about *incog-
nito.* But honor to the *belle patrie*
whose emblem is the *fleur de lys.*
Pronounce a fervent curse and damn
on who denies that war is *lam-
entable* or who won't confess
its cruelty is always *des-
picable.* Let his march be rocky
who decimates the boys in *khaki.*

Beware: such follies are the premises
of his inevitable *nemesis.*

Franglais I

Sign on Montreal garage:
NOUS FIXONS VOS FLATS.

Franglais II

Name of blue Bayliner powerboat in Montreal
harbor:
LE YES MOM BOY

Franglais III

Rock group in Montbéliard, France:

LE NO FUCK BÉBÉ

Franglais IV

Sign in window of Anglomaniac men's clothing store on the Boulevard de l'Opéra, Paris:

TRÈS ANGLAIS

BIEN SPORT

ASSEZ SNOB

PRESQUE CAD

Franglais V

This admirable example of Franco-American garble I collected personally *in situ*. It's an ad for a rock concert, a sector of life in which American English is supposed to be chic, the way restaurant menus are supposed to be more elegant in French.

YELLOW CAT et SILLY HORNETS

présentent

Agent 86 Washington Hard Core

GARLIC

FROG

DIET

Franglais VI

L'Amour

LOVING CHAIR*
Le Théâtre en Rond
Erotic Theater
62, Rue Pigalle 75009 Paris

UN ÉVÉNEMENT

SANS PRECEDENT

DANS LE SPECTACLE EROTIQUE

L'AMOUR

AU MILIEU DES

SPECTATEURS

Premiers essais en public de couples échangistes
LIFE-SHOW super choc
entre femmes, en couples, en solitaire
et en groupe strip-tease très pervers
LE HARD TRES POUSSÉ D'UN COUPLE "UP TO DATE"

*Loving chair = love seat
Life-show = nude act
Super choc = hot stuff
Le hard = porn
"Up to date" = uninhibited

—*Pariscope,* April 1994

87

The RAF Bestiary

In 1918 the British government decided to improve its chaotic system of naming military airplanes. The same machine sometimes even had several different designations, when the factory gave it one, the service in question another, and the pilots a third. Thus, the Sopwith Scout F.1 was generally known as the Camel, but to its pilots was the Camisole. (Sopwith also made a Cuckoo.)

After vast bureaucratic turmoil, the following formula was set:

Fighters

Size	Class Word
Single-seater	Insects, birds, and reptiles
Two-seater	Mammals
Three-seater	Flowers
Four-seater	Shrubs
Five-seater	Trees

Seaplanes

Size	Class word
Single-seater	River fish
Two-seater	Saltwater fish
Three-seater	Shellfish

Then it was decided to try to select the actual names from the first one or two letters of the name of the manufacturer. This engendered some conspicuously unmilitary designations, such as the de Havilland Delphinium and Dormouse,* and the Fairey Fuchsia. Boulton and Paul made a single-seater fighter that on this reasoning needed to start with BO. No such bird existed in England, so the American bobolink had to do—not a species known to those who flew the plane. The same for the Vickers Vireo, a South American finch.

Thus arose single-seater fighters with such inauspicious handles as the Snail and the Vampire, a two-seater called the Hippo, a bomber called the Rhino, and a trainer called the Baboon. Apes and Gnatsnappers lurched aloft.

Fairey Aviation, a hard case, failed to answer mail from the Air Ministry proposing names for their aircraft, so after the wimpish Fairey Fuchsia came the Fairey Salmon, a name unilaterally awarded by the ministry, but which nobody else would use. The Fairey III series never got named at all.

---

*"Wot's thet, Sahgeant?"
"A flight of Dormouses, Sah!"
"Neow, neow. Dormice, you idjit!"
"Yes, Sah!"

Rolls-Royce opposed odd avian designations for its engines. They conceded, though, that birds of prey might do. Thus the famous Merlin engine is not named, as one would suppose, for King Arthur's wizard but after a tiny hawk, the smallest raptor in Britain.

Solecisms

Leo Rosten, who as Leonard Q. Ross wrote the funniest American book, *The Education of H*Y*M*A*N K*A*P*L*A*N,* guarantees the exact accuracy of the following:

1. "Miss O'Hayer has been raising birds for many years and is credited with having the largest parakeets in the state."

2. "Mr. and Mrs. Oliver Strong request the pleasure of your presents at the marriage of their daughter. . . ."

3. Telegram from Mr. Baker, on business trip abroad, to Mrs. Baker: HAVING WONDERFUL TIME. WISH YOU WERE HER.

Extraordinary Old Inn Names

In early times inns, like tradesmen, often displayed an image on a sign, with or without a written name, or just an object, such as a boot, indicating the trade of the occupant before the house became an inn. Thus, for example, the familiar Fox when found in a city or town does not mean that the inn was frequented by foxhunters, but rather that in earlier days it was the house and shop of a furrier.

One should remember that these signs waved back and forth in all weathers and were perforce repainted at least every few generations, so that by degrees their appearance changed, sometimes completely. Also, the name was often corrupted by popular misusage.

Thus, the Andrew Mack proves to be the name of a warship, the *Andromache,* whose image had completely faded from the sign.

The Goose and Gridiron, near St. Paul's, in London, was once called the Lyre and Swan, after the emblem of the Society of Musicians, which met there. With the passage of time the swan became called a goose, and the lyre a gridiron. Later, when the inn was rebuilt, the corrupted name became the official one.

The Horseshoe and Magnet, in London, was originally called the Horse and Falcon. Later this name was distorted into Horse and Magpie, then Horse and Magnet, and finally Horseshoe and Magnet.

The Bag o' Nails was originally the Satyr and Bacchanals. The sign faded to illegibility, and the old name was deformed.

The Bull & Mouth, the name of several English inns, does not refer to a bull but to Boulogne and the mouth of the river—its harbor. This was a victory in the time of Henry VIII.

The Cat & Wheel comes from the Catherine Wheel, the wheel on which St. Catherine was martyred, which was the original sign of the Worshipful Company of Turners.

The Goat & Compasses may come from a typically Puritan sign: GOD ENCOMPASSES US.

Elephant and Castle is usually explained as Infanta de Castilla, celebrating a Spanish state visit.

The Iron Devil derives from the Arundel family crest, a swan or, in heraldry, *"hirondelle,"* which eventually turned into Iron Devil.

The Lion and Key arose when Wellington, during the Peninsular Campaign, finally captured Cuidad Rodrigo, often described as the key to Spain. There was rejoicing throughout England, and a British lion holding a key became a popular inn sign.

The Penny Come Quick is from Celtic: *pen*

(hill), *cwn* (*combe,* a vale), *wic* (house); thus, the house in the vale by the hill.

The Pig & Whistle was originally The Peg of Wassail. Old drinking vessels had internal divisions representing a pint, with a peg being set into the tankard so the drinker could see when he had reached each level. Thus, a peg, two pegs (i.e., pints), and so on; whence "take him down a peg" and the Anglo-Indian "chota (small) peg."

The Royal Mortar was previously the Royal Martyr, King Charles I.

London's Ship & Shovel began as the Ship, a tavern regularly frequented by a naval officer, Cloudsley Shovel, who, having become Admiral Sir Cloudsley Shovel, as the climax of his career ran the fleet onto the rocks in the Scilly Isles, drowning 2,000 men.

The Snob and Ghost comes from "snob," an old slang term for a shoemaker, and a ghost, pronounced "gowst," a quill used by tailors. Thus, the house was at one time probably occupied by person(s) in these trades.

The sign of the Cock and Bottle depicts a bundle of hay, once called a "cock"; thus, a hay and straw merchant. A "bottle" used to mean a smaller amount of straw. On other inn signs a cock can simply mean a rooster, usually crowing, or, particularly in the frequent Cock and Dolphin, the French heraldic cock and the heir apparent's designation, the Dauphin.

Dirty French Spoonerisms

English speakers have always enjoyed the reversed sentences (technically, metathesis) of the Rev. William A. Spooner, Warden of New College, Oxford: "Let me sew you to your sheet" for "Let me show you to your seat," or, announcing the hymn "Conquering Kings Their Titles Take" as "Kinquering Congs Their Titles Take," or angrily reproving a lazy student with "You have tasted the whole worm!"

Fewer are aware of the French equivalent, the (almost always dirty) *contrepet*. Two samples:

1. *Les laborieuses populations du Cap.*
2. *Les anglaises qui aiment le tennis en pension.*

Useful Expressions I

GREEK: *Sciopedes.* Men who hold one foot over their heads to provide shade.

HAUSA: *'Yan garkuwa.* Professional beggars living by threatening to do obscene acts unless given alms.

HINDUSTANI: *Pahárá,* a multiplication table of $4\frac{1}{2}$ times.

JAPANESE: *Uguisu no tani-watari.* (1) A nightingale jumping back and forth over a narrow alley, and thus (2) one man in bed with two women.*

Sakasa-kurage. (1) An upside-down jellyfish; (2) a one-night-stand hotel.

KIKUYU: *Komaria.* To push somebody with a stick and say "wee!"

Ruuka. To become uncircumcised.†

KURDISH: *Binêsk.* What remains of a tablet of soap, when it is nearly used up.

MALAY: *Koro.* An epidemic paranoid delusion: the patient is convinced that his penis is retracting, and that when it has vanished he will die.

MARATHI: *Avlyachi mot.* A higgledy-piggeldy assemblage with a constant tendency to fly apart.

RUSSIAN: *Vranyo.* I know he's lying. He knows that I know. I know he knows that I know.

SCOTTISH: *Taghairn.* In the highlands, divination, especially inspiration sought by lying in a bullock's hide beneath a waterfall.

---

*Poetic! J. T.
†There is quite a literature on this important conception.

Kurdish : Binêsk. What remains of a tablet of soap when it is nearly used up

SESUTO: *Malito.* Something a person lets fall and his cousin can pick up and keep if the owner does not say *"ngaele."*

SINHALESE: *Akshauhiai.* An army consisting of 21,870 elephants, 21,870 chariots, 65,610 horses and 109,350 foot soldiers.

SPANISH: *Orejon.* Pull by the ear; preserved peach; scion of ancient Peruvian nobility.

SPANISH: *Pechando.* Two mounted gauchos charge 200 yards or so directly into each other, crash, fall, remount, and repeat until one is incapacitated or dead.

SWAHILI: *Hatinafsi.* When a person acts without consulting anybody because he thinks he may be persuaded not to do it.*

*Sources:

Aristotle. *Dictionary of the Hausa Language* by R. C. Abraham (London, 2nd ed., 1962.)

The Student's Romanised Practical Dictionary (Allahabad, 1941.)

Japanese in Action by Jack Seward (Tokyo, 1968.)

Kikuyu-English Dictionary T. G. Benson, ed. (Oxford, 1964.)

A Kurdish-English Dictionary by T. Wahby and C. J. Edmonds (Oxford, 1966.)

Stedman's Medical Dictionary.

The Arya-Bushan School Dictionary by Shridhar Ganesh Vaze, B.A. (1928).

Collins Dictionary of English.

Sesuto-English Vocabulary, Societé des Missions Evangeliques de Paris. (Cape Town, 1904.)

Sinhalese-English Dictionary, edited for the University of Ceylon by M. D. Ratnasuriya and P. B. F. Wijeratne. (Colombo, 1949.)

Harrap's Concise Spanish Dictionary.

The *Times Literary Supplement.*

A Standard Swahili-English Dictionary. (Oxford, 1939.)

Useful Expressions II

The Walk

You hear the bird's gurgling?

For to Ride a Horse

Your pistols are its loads?

No; I forgot to buy gun-powder and balls. Let us prick. Go us more fast never I was seen a so much bad beast; she will not nor to bring forward neither put back.

Take care that he not give you a foot kick's.

Then he kicks for that I look? Sook here if I knew to tame him.

For Embarking One's Self

Don't you fear the privateers!

I jest of them; my vessel is armed in man of war, I have a vigilant and courageous equipage, and the ammunitions don't want me its.

Never have not you not done wreck?

That is arrived me twice.

Diseases

The scrofulas	The whitlow
The megrime	The vomitory

With a Laundress

Who that be too washed, too many soaped, and the shirts put through the buck.

You may be sure; never I do else.

With a Hair Dresser

Comb-me quickly; don't put me so much pomatum.

What news tell me? all hairs dresser are newsmonger.

Idiotisms and Proverbs

He sin in trouble water.
A horse baared don't look him the tooth.
The stone as roll not heap up not foam.

—Pedro Carlino's *New Guide of the Conversation in Portuguese and English,* 1883

Useful Expressions III

The word for *piano* in Solomon Islands pidgin English is BOKKIS YUPALA HITTIM I TOK:

"Box you (you fella) hit him he talks."

Crazy Monikers

The English delight in double-barrelled names. Sometimes a husband hyphenated his wife's surname if she brought substantial property to the marriage. Then sometimes a double-barrel would marry another double-barrel, producing, as it were, Infant Double-Barrel-Double-Barrel, or even Infant Multiple-Double-Barrel.

1. Sir Ranulph Twisleton-Wykeham-Fiennes, explorer.
2. Admiral the Hon. Sir Reginald Aylmer Ranfurley Plunkett-Ernle-Erle-Drax, participant in the Battle of Jutland; British Military Mission to Russia, 1939.
3. The Honourable Alexander Hovell-Thurlow-Cumming-Bruce, Durham.
4. Brigadier Dermot Hugh Blundell-Hollinshead-Blundell, c/o BFPO 26, London.

5. Lady Caroline Jemima Temple-Nugent-Chandos-Brydges-Grenville, 1858–1946.

6. Major Leone Sextus Denys Oswolf Fraudatifilius Tollmache-Tollemache-de Orellana-Plantagenet-Tollemache-Tollemache, 1884–1917.

7. Lyulph Ydwallo Odin Nestor Egbert Lyonel Toedmag Hugh Erchenwyne Saxon Esa Cromwell Orma Nevill Dysart Plantagenet Tollemache-Tollemache, Tauranga, New Zealand. (*Burke's Peerage and Baronetage*)

INDEX